THEBIBLE
IN HEADLINES

A one or two line heading for every chapter in the Bible

FOR REFERENCE AND MEMORIZATION

Peter Barker
edited by Helen Barker
2017

First Printing: 1985

ISBN 978-0-9957668-0-8

Cover design: James Crawford

Published by Helen Barker, West Sussex, United Kingdom
http://bibleinheadlines.wixsite.com/bihblog

Table of Contents

HOW TO USE THE BIBLE IN HEADLINES

Use these headlines with your Bible reading
Get daily Bible reading notes and never miss your daily time of prayer and Bible reading. Turn to the headlines for the book you are studying, and use them to see where the day's passage fits in to the whole book.

Read the Bible one chapter a day with the corresponding headline
Underline or highlight any verses that particularly stand out to you. The headline will also help you to remember what you have read. If you read a chapter a day for three years and three months you will complete the whole Bible.

Read through two pages of this book every day
There are 62 pages in total, so you can read 2 a day each month. In months of less than 31 days you can omit one or more of the date charts.

Learn the names & order of Bible books & events
Use the Table of Contents and date charts to learn how people, places and events fit together.

Examples of abbreviations used in this book:

cov^t	covenant	M	Moses	S	Solomon
D	David	M^t	Mount	S	south
d	dies	N	Nehemiah	v	against (vs)
E	east	N	north	vv	verses
&c	etc./others	P^l	Paul	W	west
J^m } Jerusalem		P^t	Peter	X^n	Christian
Jer^m		qn^s	questions	X^t	Christ
J	Jeremiah	R	River	yrs	years

Preface

This book began life as a result of my father's personal discipline of Bible study and memorization. He discovered the benefit of becoming familiar with the books of the Bible, and the stories and truths contained in them. As a great expounder and evangelist, he knew the importance of memorizing scripture and knowing how to find passages in the Bible. He compiled this summary of key points from each chapter in the Bible, in the hope that it would be of help to others.

I began re-working it, with his editorial input, several years ago, and was encouraged by others who had seen the original to complete the task, following my father's passing in May 2016. I have also added an appendix of 'Helpful verses' compiled by my mother many years ago.

My hope and prayer is that 'The Bible in Headlines' will help you as you read and study the Word of God. There is no substitute for reading the Bible itself – the intention of this book is simply to be a tool to help you locate, learn and remember scripture, so that you may gain a richer knowledge of God and His Word.

Helen Barker, 2017

All Scripture is God-breathed and is useful for teaching, rebuking, correcting and training in righteousness, so that the man of God may be thoroughly equipped for every good work.

2 Timothy 3:16-17

DIVISIONS OF THE OLD AND NEW TESTAMENTS

OLD TESTAMENT

LAW and HISTORY

Genesis

Exodus

Leviticus

Numbers

Deuteronomy

HISTORY

-in the promised land

Joshua

Judges

Ruth

-the kingdoms

1&2 Samuel

1&2 Kings

1&2 Chronicles

-the exile and return

Ezra

Nehemiah

Esther

POETRY

Job

Psalms

Proverbs

Ecclesiastes

Song of Songs

PROPHECY

"Major"

Isaiah

Jeremiah

Lamentations

Ezekiel

Daniel

"Minor"

Hosea

Joel

Amos

Obadiah

Jonah

Micah

Nahum

Habakkuk

Zephaniah

Haggai

Zechariah

Malachi

NEW TESTAMENT

HISTORY

Matthew

Mark

Luke

John

Acts

LETTERS from PAUL

-to seven churches

Romans

1&2 Corinthians

Galatians

Ephesians

Philippians

Colossians

1&2 Thessalonians

-to three individuals

1&2 Timothy

Titus

Philemon

OTHER LETTERS

Hebrews

James

1&2 Peter

1,2&3 John

Jude

PROPHECY

Revelation

GENESIS 1 – 24

ABRAHAM

GENESIS 25 – 50

JACOB

JOSEPH

EXODUS 1 – 19

1 new king's cruelty; he tells midwives "kill babies"

2 Moses: childhood, kills Egyptian, flees to Midian

3 Moses called at burning bush; God's name "I AM"

4 signs to Moses; Aaron helps; return to Egypt

5 "let my people go"; bricks without straw; prayer

6 Moses told "lead Israel out of Egypt"; Levi's clan

7 Aaron's stick; 10 plagues – *1* rivers to blood

8 *2* frogs from Nile; *3* gnats; *4* flies; (king stubborn)

9 *5* cattle disease; *6* boils; *7* hail

10 (king still stubborn); *8* locusts; *9* darkness

11 Moses warns Pharaoh that first-born will die

12 Passover; *10* first-born die; Jews leave Egypt

13 festival of unleavened bread; first-born
   are God's; pillars of cloud and fire

14 Egyptian army pursues, drowned in Red Sea

15 songs of Moses & Miriam; bitter water at Marah

16 God sends manna and quail

17 water from rock; Amalek beaten – Moses' arms

18 Jethro's visit; Moses delegates work to judges

19 Israel at Sinai prepares for covenant with God

10 PLAGUES (chapters 7–12)

EGPYT TO SINAI (chapters 14–18)

EXODUS 20 – 40

20 10 commandments; people's fear; rules for altars

21 laws on slavery; acts of violence, compensation

22 compensation; seduction; aliens; loans

23 justice; 7th year, day; 3 festivals; protecting angel

24 covenant ratified with blood; 70 elders see God

25 offerings for tent: covenant-box, table, lamp

26 woven coverings, clasps, frames, curtain

27 altar; enclosure of curtains; oil for the lamp

28 priests' clothes – ephod, breast-piece, &c

29 sacrifices for priests' ordination; daily offerings

30 incense altar; tent upkeep tax; basin; oil; incense

31 Bezalel & Oholiab; sabbath is sign of God's rest

DESIGN OF TENT

32 gold bull; Moses' prayer; Levites kill 3,000

33 "leave Sinai" – "go with us", M sees God's face

34 2nd stone tablets, cov't renewed, M's face shines

LAPSE & RESTORATION

35 sabbath; offerings & craftsmen for making tent

36 more than enough gifts; the tent constructed

37 covenant-box, table, lampstand, incense & altar

38 altar, bronze basin, enclosure; weights of metals

39 making priests' clothes; the work completed

40 tent set up; cloud by day, fire by night

MAKING TENT

LEVITICUS

OFFERINGS

PRIESTS

RITUAL CLEANNESS

NUMBERS 1 – 21

1 12 tribes numbered; Levites appointed

2 camp positions E, S, W, N of Tent of Meeting

3 Levites' duties; Levites work in place of firstborn

4 Levites' duties listed by their families

5 repayment for wrong; test of wives' faithfulness

6 law for Nazirite vow; form of blessing

7 tribes' offerings for dedication of altar

8 lamps lit; Levites' consecration, years of service

9 2nd Passover; ritual uncleanness; cloud, fire

10 trumpets; leaving Sinai; Hobab; ark 3 days ahead

11 grumbling punished; 70 elders prophesy; quail

12 Miriam and Aaron criticize Moses' marriage

MOVE

13 12 spies go to Canaan and report back

14 grumbling; Moses' prayer; defeat at Hormah

15 sacrifices; Sabbath breaker stoned; tassels

16 earthquake kills rebels Korah, Dathan & Abiram

17 Aaron's staff sprouts, proving his authority

18 priests' and Levites' duties and privileges

19 ashes of red cow for cleansing ritual uncleanness

20 Miriam d; Moses strikes rock at Meribah for water,

king of Edom refuses passage; Aaron dies

38 YEARS AT KADESH

21 1st victory in Canaan; bronze snake; Sihon, Og

NUMBERS 22 – 36

ON THE PLAINS OF MOAB

DEUTERONOMY 1 – 8

DEUTERONOMY 9 – 34

1ST COLLECTION

2ND

3RD

JOSHUA

JUDGES

1   Canaan partly conquered by various tribes
2   angel at Bochim; Joshua dies; idolatry punished
3   remaining nations; judges Othniel, Ehud, Shamgar
4   Deborah and Barak defeat Sisera & Canaanites
5   song of Deborah and Barak
6   Midian oppresses Israel; Gideon called
7   Gideon's small army; trumpets, jars, torches
8   Midian pursued; Gideon makes an idol
                                             GIDEON
9   Abimelech kills Gideon's 70 sons; his reign
10 Tola, Jair; Ammonites oppress Israel
11 Jephthah defeats Ammon, sacrifices his daughter
12 Jeph attacks Ephraim: "Shibboleth" password
13 angel promises birth of Samson; he'll be a Nazirite
14 Samson's bride reveals riddle, so he kills 30
15 S destroys harvest with torches, foxes; jawbone   SAMSON
16 prostitute Delilah betrays Samson's secret
17 Micah makes an idol, employs Levite as priest
18 Danites seize Laish with both priest and idol
19 men of Gibeah rape a traveller's companion
20 Benjamin destroyed as a punishment
21 massacre of Jabesh provides wives for remnant

RUTH

1   widow from Moab moves to Israel with m-in-law
2   Ruth gleans corn in field of Boaz at Bethlehem
3   Ruth sleeps at Boaz's threshing floor
4   Boaz performs custom and marries Ruth

years before Christ	UNITED ISRAELITE KINGDOM		Prophets
	c 1050 reign of SAUL	*1 Samuel 10 – 31*	Gad
1000	c 1010 reign of DAVID	*2 Samuel 1 – 24* *1 Chronicles 11 – 29*	Nathan
	c 970 reign of SOLOMON	*1 Kings 1 – 11* *2 Chronicles 1 – 9*	

950

TWO ISRAELITE KINGDOMS

JUDAH (south)	*1 Kings*	*2 Chronicles*	ISRAEL (north)	
931 REHOBOAM Shemaiah	*12-14*	*10-13*	931 JEROBOAM I	
913 ABIJAH	*15*			
911 ASA		*14*	909 NADAB	
	16	*14-16*	908 BAASHA	
900				Jehu
			886 ELAH	
			885 ZIMRI / TIBNI / OMRI	
	17-20		874 AHAB	
872 JEHOSHAPHAT Elijah Obadiah				Micaiah
853 JEHORAM	*22*		853 AHAZIAH	
850	*2 Kings 1-6*		852 JORAM	Elisha
		21		
841 AHAZIAH	*8-10*	*22*	841 JEHU	
841 ATHALIAH	*11*			
835 JOASH	*12-13*	*24*		
			814 JEHOAHAZ	

Note: Prophets are shown in *italics* alongside the kingdom and/or time period they are most associated with, although some prophesied to both kingdoms or to neither.

12

	JUDAH (south)	2 Kings	2 Chronicles	ISRAEL (north)	Prophets

TWO ISRAELITE KINGDOMS   *Prophets*

	JUDAH (south)	*2 Kings*	*2 Chronicles*	ISRAEL (north)	
800					
	796 AMAZIAH	*13-14*	*25*	798 JEHOASH	
	792 UZZIAH (AZARIAH)	*14-15*	*26*	793 JEROBOAM II	*Jonah*
					Amos
					Hosea
				753 ZECHARIAH	
				752 SHALLUM	
750	750 JOTHAM			752 MENAHEM / PEKAH	
		Micah	*27*	742 PEKAHIAH	
		Isaiah			
	735 AHAZ	*16-17*			
		Oded	*28*	732 HOSHEA	
				722 Fall of Samaria	
				EXILE IN ASSYRIA	
	715 HEZEKIAH	*18-20*	*29-32*	Many Israelites taken into exile in Assyria, Halah, Gozan & Media	
700					
	697 MANASSEH	*21*	*33*		
650					
	642 AMON				
		Nahum			
	640 JOSIAH	*22*	*34-35*		
		Zephaniah			*Jeremiah*
					Obadiah?
	609 JEHOAHAZ		*36*		
	609 JEHOIAKIM	*23-24*			
		Habakkuk			
	604 Battle of Carchemish				
600					
	598 JEHOIACHIN				
	597 ZEDEKIAH				
	c 586 Fall of Jerusalem	*25*			*Ezekiel*
	EXILE IN BABYLONIA				*Daniel*
	Many Jews taken into exile in Babylonia				
550					

1 SAMUEL

SAMUEL & SAUL

SAUL & DAVID

2 SAMUEL

ABSALOM

1 KINGS

1	Adonijah tries to seize throne; Solomon king	
2	David instructs S, dies; S kills Adonijah, Joab	
3	S's marriage, prayer, & wise judgement	*2 Ch 1*
4	S's admin, empire, wealth, cavalry, wisdom	
5	S plans Temple; trade with Hiram of Tyre	*2*
6	S builds Temple; dimensions, furnishings	*3*
7	S's palace; Huram makes columns, sea, &c	*3,4*
8	cov^t box to Temple, S's prayer, dedication	*5-7*
9	God answers S; S's trading & construction	*7,8*
10	Q^n of Sheba's visit; S's wealth, fame, cavalry	*9*
11	S's polygamy, idolatry, enemies, death	*9*

(SOLOMON)

12	N kingd^m secedes; *Jboam's* golden calves	*10-11*
13	prophet warns *Jboam,* killed by lion; *J's* priests	
14	Ahijah warns *Jboam;* Rehoboam of Judah	*11-12*
15	Abijah; Asa's reform; *Nadab, Baasha*	*13-16*
16	*Baasha, Elah, Zimri, Omri, Ahab*	

(DIVISION)

17	Elijah & drought, widow of Zarephath & son
18	Elijah to *Ahab;* Elijah & Baal prophets at Carmel
19	Elijah to Sinai; the "small voice"; call of Elisha
20	*Ahab* defeats Benhadad of Syria, but is rebuked
21	Naboth killed; *Ahab* takes his vineyard
22	*Ahab* rejects warning, dies; Jehoshaphat; *Ahaziah*

(AHAB & ELIJAH)

Note: *names of kings of northern kingdoms are in italics*

2 KINGS

ELISHA

KINGS OF JUDAH & ISRAEL

1 CHRONICLES

1 Adam, Noah, Abraham, Ishmael, Isaac

2 Israel, Judah 3 David, Solomon 4 Judah, Simeon

3 Reuben, Gad; defeat of the Hagrites

6 Levi, Aaron; Temple singers; Levites' settlements

7 Issachar Benj[n] Naphtali Manasseh Ephraim Asher

8 Benjamin, Saul

9 returned exiles; family of Saul

10 Philistine victory; Saul and sons *1 Sam 31*

11 David captures Zion; chief soldiers *2 Sam 5, 23*

12 David's supporters at Ziklag, Hebron

13 cov[t] box moved from Kiriath Jearim to Gath *6*

14 Hiram of Tyre; D's ch[n]; he defeats Philistines *5*

15 David moves covenant box to Jerusalem *6*

16 song (= Ps 105, 96); Levites lead worship

17 David plans to build Temple; his prayer *7*

18 David's victories and administration *8*

19 Hanun's insult; Ammon and Syria defeated *10*

20 D captures Rabbah, kills Philistine giants *12, 21*

21 epidemic after census stops in Jerusalem *24*

22 Temple site, materials; "help Solomon"

23 Levites' duties; Gershom, Kohath, Merari families

24 priests' duties; their 24 family groups

25 musicians: Asaph, Jeduthun, Heman families

26 Temple guards, treasurers, and administration

27 administrators for each month and tribe

28 David hands over building of Temple to Solomon

29 gifts for building; D praises God, Solomon king

GENEALOGIES

DAVID

2 CHRONICLES 1 – 24

2 CHRONICLES 25 – 36

KINGS OF JUDAH

EZRA

BUILDING TEMPLE

NEHEMIAH

1 news from Jerusalem; Nehemiah prays
2 king gives N permiss^n to go to J^m, sends escort
3 how rebuilding the walls was organised
4 critics mock and oppose, so workers are armed
5 rich forego claims on poor; N's simple life-style
6 foes fail to trap or frighten N; walls finished

BUILDING WALLS

7 officials appointed; list of returned exiles (= Ezra 2)
8 weeping as Ezra reads law; festival of shelters
9 prayer recalling Israel's sins & God's faithfulness
10 the people promise to keep the law
11 list of leading citizens of J^m, nearby settlements
12 returning priests and Levites; dedication of wall
13 N's reforms – support of Levites, keeping sabbath

ESTHER

1 Xerxes deposes queen Vashti for disobeying him
2 Esther queen; Mordecai reveals plot *v* king
3 Haman hates Mordecai, plans to destroy Jews
4 Mordecai persuades Esther to intervene
5 Esther's dinner; Haman makes gallows for Mordecai
6 Haman forced to honour Mordecai
7 Esther reveals Haman's plot; Haman hanged
8 Jews given authority to resist their enemies
9 Jews destroy their enemies; festival of Purim
10 Xerxes' achievements; Mordecai second in rank

JOB 1 – 21

1 God lets Satan destroy Job's wealth and family

2 Job suffers from boils; three friends visit him

3 JOB: I wish I had never been born

4 ELIPHAZ: only wicked suffer; can man be pure?

5 seek God; he wounds but he also heals

6 JOB: let God kill me! My friends talk nonsense

7 why does God bother to torment me?

8 BILDAD: repent! God punishes sinners, godless

9 JOB: even the innocent can't argue with creator

10 God's justice pursues me without pity

11 ZOPHAR: you deserve worse things; repent!

12 JOB: we all know God creates, sustains, destroys

13 don't defend God; let *him* tell me my crimes

14 is there life after death?

15 ELIPHAZ: you're wrong! all sin and are punished

16 JOB: tho' innocent, I'm a target of God & man

17 I'm misunderstood; my only hope is to die

18 BILDAD: wicked are sure to lose riches, health

19 JOB: God destroys me, yet I shall see him!

20 ZOPHAR: wicked may prosper but will fall

21 JOB: no! many sinners do prosper till death

1ST CYCLE OF SPEECHES

2ND CYCLE

JOB 22 – 42

22 ELIPHAZ: you exploited poor; abandon riches

23 JOB: where is God, that I may present my case?

24 why doesn't God step in to stop oppression?

    ZOPHAR: God *does* punish the oppressor

25 BILDAD: man cannot be righteous before God

26 creator's greatness is beyond man's grasp

27 JOB: I'm innocent; ZOPH: God strikes sinners

28 we dig for gold, but find wisdom only with God

29 JOB: I recall my former reputation and dignity

30 now youths mock me, God punishes me

31 yet I've been honest, moral, generous, frank

32 ELIHU: you're *all* wrong; now listen to me

33 all God does is for our good, to help us repent

34 God is not unjust; he punishes sinners; confess!

35 though insignificant, your case is before God

36 don't be bitter – God teaches us through suffering

37 storm and weather reveal God's glory

38 GOD: Job, look at creation – light, storm, stars,

39   animals, birds – could you create them?

40 you can't argue with the hippopotamus's maker

41 you're helpless before the crocodile (Leviathan)

42 Job repents; God restores him and rebukes his friends

3RD CYCLE

ELIHU

PSALMS 1 – 26

1   secure in God's Word? or blown off course? **Bk 1**
2   God's chosen king will rule the earth
3   many enemies but I don't fear, for God protects me
4   insults don't disturb our peace, joy or sleep
5   God protects faithful worshippers *v* enemies
6   I'm worn out and miserable, yet I trust God
7   I'm innocent – defend me against my attackers
8   creator has entrusted his world to humanity!
9   praise God, who saves us from our enemies
10   God punishes shameless persecutors
11   I don't run away, for God deals with my foes
12   help, none are good! God *will* help oppressed
13   "how long will God forget me?" yet I trust him
14   godless evildoers are just ignorant fools (= Ps 53)
15   characteristics of one who worships God
16   God keeps me secure, both now and in death
17   you know I'm innocent – protect me from foes
18   David's song of victory over Saul (= 2 Samuel 22)
19   God revealed to us in creation and in Scripture
20   prayer for the king before a battle
21   thanksgiving for the king after a victory
22   suffering from sickness and foes, I praise God
23   the Lord is my loving shepherd, guide, and host
24   God enters his holy place; who may enter with him?
25   I'm a sinner; so I need you to save me
26   I'm innocent; but I need you to save me

PSALMS 27 – 50

27 trust in God and love for God's house banish fear

28 I praise God for he hears my prayer for retribution

29 God's voice in storm and thunder (part = Ps 96)

30 I rejoice because God saved me from a serious illness

31 lonely, persecuted, but God heard my prayer

32 sin caused misery, confession brought forgiveness

33 fear him who created world and rules all nations

34 I found out how good God is; so can you!

35 false accusers attack me; stop them, save me!

36 wicked people's deep sin, God's constant love!

37 don't envy the wicked – claim God's promises

38 my sin has made me suffer; now I repent

39 a dying man searches for the meaning of his life

40 in trouble, I recall past mercies (part = Ps 70)

41 sick, sinful, maligned disloyally, I still trust God

42-43 exiled, miserable, suffering & in pain, | **Bk 2**

I seek God & long to worship in the Temple

44 help, God! don't abandon your loyal people

45 wedding song for king, bride, & (v 17) Messiah

46 the mighty God who stops wars is our refuge

47 clap for our God, the God of all nations

48 there's joy in God's holy city; enemies fear it

49 you can't take riches with you when you die

50 sacrifice is good but hypocrisy belies it

SONS OF KORAH

PSALMS 51 – 75

PSALMS 76 – 100

76 don't try to resist our victorious God

77 two reactions to trouble – despair, praise

78 history of Israel's failure and God's mercy

79 we're invaded, Temple sacked, God help us

80 save Israel, your neglected vine, from enemies

81 during festival, God speaks but Israel won't listen

82 God condemns unjust judges

83 let our enemies fall – and recognise God!

ASAPH

84 I long to be in God's house and presence

85 God has forgiven us and will give us a new start

86 under attack, I expect God to answer my prayer

87 all of us belong to God's city, Zion

88 a lifelong invalid despairs but prays daily

89 I claim God's promises to David tho' I feel rejected

90 eternal creator, make my 70 yrs worth it   **Bk 4**

91 God protects those who really know him

92 praise for prosperity; evildoers scattered

93 God's greatness likened to the ocean

94 God seems slow to punish, but his justice triumphs

95 praise our ruler and maker, don't try his patience

96 sing new song, all nations & creation (= 1Ch 16)

97 God rules all creation and upholds good people

98 people & creation, make music to God our judge!

99 our mighty, holy king answers prayer

100 praise God who made us, in his Temple

PSALMS 101 – 125

PSALMS 126 – 150

126 take us back home safely as you did once before!

127 useless to make plans & leave God out of them

128 blessing on individual, family, & nation

129 persecution has made me bitter *v* my enemies

130 hope of forgiveness even in depths of despair

131 I give up selfish ambition & humbly trust in God

132 David's vow to build Temple, & God's promise

133 the joy of living together in harmony

134 call to an all-night of praise and prayer

SONGS OF ASCENTS

135 God has power, idols don't (part = Ps 115)

136 God's enduring love in events of Israel's history

137 exiles, too sad to sing, predict Babylon's fall

138 Lord you're utterly reliable; kings will praise you

139 God made me, knows all about me, cares for me

140 I plead for help; pour hot coals on my enemies!

141 keep me from sin; protect me against traps

142 I cry to God for help; no one else cares for me

143 I've lost hope; 11 prayers in vv 6-12

144 you save me in war; give prosperity in peace

145 I tell others God is good and meets our needs

146 Praise God the best friend – he helps the needy

147 Praise God, he restores exiles, sends rain, gives laws

148 Praise God, you angels, stars, animals, & all people!

149 Praise God for victory, and keep on fighting evil!

150 Praise God with all kinds of musical instrument!

PROVERBS 1 – 24

1 the purpose of proverbs; don't neglect wisdom!

2 seek wisdom – to save you from sin & wicked people

3 trust God, welcome correction, help others

4 son, avoid evil people, take Dad seriously

5 warning *v* immorality; be faithful to your wife

6 don't guarantee debts; laziness; 7 things; *v* adultery

7 how an immoral woman seduces a young man

8 wisdom appeals to men; she was created first

9 wisdom and stupidity invite guests to a meal

*In chapters 10–29 the first item in each summary
is the theme of verse 1*

10 wise son, laziness; right speaking 18-21, 31-32

11 dishonesty 1-6, 10; generosity 17, 24-26

12 correction; right speaking 6, 13, 16-19, 22-23

13 father's correction 1, 24; wealth 7-8, 11, 21-25

14 women's wisdom; folly and wisdom contrasted

15 answers; speaking 1-7, 23-28; contentment 16-17

16 plans 1-3, 9, 33; pride 5, 18-19; speech 13, 23, 28

17 dry crust, strife 1, 14, 19; fools 7, 10, 12, 16, 21

18 relationships; speaking 4-7, 19-21; friends 19, 24

19 poverty 1-7, 17, 22; anger 11-12, 19

20 drink; laziness, honesty, trade, profit

21 the king's mind; righteous & wicked contrasted

22 wealth, poverty 1-2, 4, 7, 9, 16, 22; 4 prohibitions

23 greed; more prohibitions; drunkenness described

24 envy; wisdom and folly; justice, honesty, laziness

SOLOMON'S PROVERBS (1ST BOOK)

PROVERBS 25 – 31

25 Solomon's proverbs; homely comparisons
26 fools 1-12; laziness 13-16; lies and gossip 17-28
27 don't boast of tomorrow; friends, relationships
28 the wicked run away; the poor 3, 6, 8, 11, 27
29 stubbornness; social and political principles
30 *Agur:* knowing God; 2 requests; 5 groups of 4
31 *Lemuel:* women, wine, justice; the capable wife

(2ND BOOK)

ECCLESIASTES

1 life and history are a meaningless cycle
2 pleasure and toil are both futile; at last we all die
3 "a time"; God in control; men are like animals
4 futility of oppression, toil, loneliness, kingly rule
5 vows to God; riches don't satisfy; real enjoyment
6 riches and wisdom prove pointless at last
7 life's disappointments and inconsistencies
8 obey the king; the problem of unpunished sin
9 all suffer same fate; enjoy life! wisdom better than folly
10 proverbs of politics, government, and planning
11 proverbs of prudence, life, and youth
12 remember God before old age sets in; fear God!

SONG OF SONGS

1 a bride goes to the palace and talks love to the king
2 the bride praises her lover; he pays her a visit
3 she seeks lover; Solomon carried in procession
4 the lover praises bride's physical beauty
5 the lover's brief visit; bride describes his beauty
6 the lover describes bride's lovely face
7 lover describes bride's body from feet to head
8 thoughts of love; the lover and his bride united

ISAIAH 1 – 23

1 God warns *v* sin, vain sacrifices; he'll purify, save

2 eventual peace and punishment of pride, idolatry

3 future corruption and chaos; *v* luxurious living

4 Jerusalem to be restored; God's glory over Mt Zion

5 song of the vineyard; *v* excess of riches & drink

6 God calls Isaiah; nation won't understand till exiled

7 Syria & Israel threaten Jer^m; the sign of Immanuel

8 Isaiah's son has prophetic name "Assyria will
   take plunder" but Assyria's doomed; *v* mediums

9 child born to be king; stubborn Israel will burn

10 Assyria, God's instrument, will be punished

11 Branch from "stump"; wolf & lamb; exiles' return

12 a psalm for the returned exiles

13 *Babylon* will become a haunt of desert animals

14 king of Bab^n falls to the dead; *v Assyria, Philistines*

15 *Moab*'s sudden fall, suffering, and refugees

16 proud, fertile Moab will fall in exactly 3 years

17 *Syria* and *Israel* will fall because they forgot God

18 *Sudanese* will be defeated and bring gifts

19 *Egypt* will turn to God after drought & civil war

20 naked prophet predicts naked Egyptian captives

21 *Babylon*'s abrupt fall; messages for *Edom, Arabia*

22 *J^m*'s fall described; Eliakim to replace Shebna

23 *Tyre* and *Sidon* traders fall; Tyre forgotten 70 yrs

MESSAGES FOR THE NATIONS

ISAIAH 24 – 39

24 God will punish earth by destruction, chaos

25 song of praise, food for poor; no more death

26 song of trust in God; dead shall live

27 Israel a vineyard; city desolate; exiles return

28 Israel's rulers, Judah's prophets drunk; a Stone

29 Jer^m doomed; blind religion; hope of restoration

30 don't rely on Egypt; God will show the way

31 Egypt can't save, God can; turn back to him

32 just king and rulers; women of Jerusalem warned

33 God's power to save Jerusalem, destroy enemies

34 God condemns enemies; Edom left to wild birds

35 desert will bloom, exiles will return by Holy Road

36 Assyria takes Judah's cities, their official's insults

37 Isaiah: "don't fear, God will defend us"

38 Hezekiah's illness; his lament & song of praise

39 Hezekiah unwisely welcomes Babylon envoys

HEZEKIAH

ISAIAH 40 – 66

40 prepare God's way; his power in creation
41 who controls history? not idols made by men!
42 *Servant Song 1;* God will save his blind people
43 God promises to bring back exiles from Babylon
44 folly of man-made idols; God forgives, creates
45 Cyrus called to help Israel; clay and potter; return!
46 Babylon's man-made gods have to be carried!
47 Babylon felt secure, but will fall despite magic
48 God predicts future, has plans for exiles' return
49 *Servant Song 2;* God will restore Jerusalem
50 *Servant Song 3 – the servant's obedience*
51 "don't fear; enemies will drink cup of suffering"
52 good news of return from exile; *Servant Song 4 –*
53 *the punishment we deserved fell on the Servant*
54 God loves Israel though it's like an unfaithful wife
55 turn to God – his mercy is free, his word is sure
56 rewards of obeying law are for all nations
57 idolatry condemned; high and lofty one forgives
58 the kind of fast God wants is social justice
59 sin separates from God; confess and he will heal
60 Jerusalem, arise, shine! Israel's future prosperity
61 sent to give good news to the poor; prosperity
62 Jer^m restored for ever; make a highway for God
63 God the avenger; where is God's former power
64 Father, you were angry with us; won't you help?
65 idolaters punished, a few saved; new creation
66 *v* false worship; God will soon bring prosperity

years before Christ	JEWS IN EXILE IN BABYLONIA	*Prophets*

PERSIAN RULE

550

538 Edict of Cyrus allows Jews to return

537 Foundations of new Temple laid

520   *Haggai / Zechariah*

500   *Joel?*

458 Ezra arrives in Jerusalem

445 Nehemiah governor: walls of Jerusalem restored

433   *Malachi*

400

GREEK RULERS

333 Alexander the Great establishes Greek rule in Palestine

323

300

Palestine ruled by the Ptolemies, descendants of one of
Alexander's generals, who had conquered Egypt

200   198

Palestine ruled by the Seleucids, descendants of another of
Alexander's generals, who had conquered Syria

JEWISH INDEPENDENCE

166 Revolt of Judas Maccabaeus

Palestine ruled by the Hasmoneans, members of Judas' family and
descendants

100

ROME APPOINTS PUPPET KINGS

63 Roman general Pompey captures Jerusalem

37 Rome appoints Herod the Great

c 6 Birth of Jesus

4 Rome appoints Tetrarchs in Judea, Galilee, Iturea

JEREMIAH 1 – 25

1 Jeremiah's call; signs of almond, boiling pot
2 Israel abandons God, seeks help from Egypt &c
3 after false repentance, Israel must truly repent
4 repent! coming invasion from north predicted
5 stubborn Israel is bound to be punished
6 escape from invasion! prophets lie, "All is well"
7 injustice and idolatry make mockery of worship
8 God asks, "Why don't you repent?"; J's sorrow
9 treacherous Judah ruined; boast you know God
10 idols compared to Creator; exile, plea for mercy
11 Judah has broken covenant; plot *v* Jeremiah's life
12 wicked prosper; God will punish & restore if they learn
13 linen belt; wineskins; exile – Israel won't change
14 drought; prophets tell lies; plea for mercy
15 4 destroyers; J persecuted; repent & God will restore
16 J not to marry or mourn; after exile, you'll return
17 curse & blessing; deceitful heart; heal me; keep sabbath
18 potter; people forget God; another plot *v* J
19 Jeremiah breaks jar, predicts ruin of Jerusalem
20 J replies to Pashur; curses day he was born
21 king enquires of J; there's no hope – surrender!
22 don't oppress; fate of 2 kings & of Jerusalem
23 bad kings, righteous Branch, lying prophets & oracles
24 good figs = exiles; bad figs = those staying in Jm
25 70 yrs' exile in Babylon; God's anger on nations

PROPHECIES AGAINST JUDAH & JERUSALEM

JEREMIAH 26 – 52

26	elders and officials resist threats to kill Jeremiah
27	J carries ox yoke – "submit to king of Babylon"
28	Jeremiah rebukes Hananiah for false prophecy
29	Jeremiah's letters to exiles and to Shemaiah
30	after exile God will restore Jerusalem, give ruler
31	exiles will return; God's mercy & a new covenant
32	J buys a field; J^m will burn; promise of restoration
33	Jerusalem will prosper again; the future king
34	J warns king; condemns treatment of slaves
35	Rechabites refuse offer of wine, obey father
36	Baruch writes prophecies; king burns scroll
37	Egyptian army will return; Jeremiah imprisoned
38	Ethiopian rescues J from well; king asks advice
39	Nebuchadnezzar captures Jerusalem, sets J free
40	J stays with Gedaliah, governor of Judah
41	Ishmael murders Gedaliah, then escapes
42	Jeremiah warns Johanan against going to Egypt
43	Johanan goes to Egypt; Neb will conquer Egypt
44	Jews in Egypt worship "queen of heaven"
45	"Baruch, don't expect special treatment!"
46	Bab^n conquers *Egypt* at Carchemish, Israel saved
47	*Philistines* will be destroyed from north
48	*Moab* to be destroyed; go & live in the rocks
49	*Ammon, Edom, Damascus, Kedar, Hazor, Elam*
50	*Babylon* to be destroyed; Israel must run away
51	Babylon the destroyer will be destroyed
52	Zedekiah rebels, siege, Jerusalem falls 587, exile

PROPHECIES AND NARRATIVES

MESSAGES FOR THE NATIONS

LAMENTATIONS

1 Jerusalem punished; "no one to comfort me"
2 city and Temple in ruins; prophets lied! weep!
3 I lament – but there may be hope if we repent
4 siege made us cannibals; priests, leaders blamed
5 daily life under enemy occupation

EZEKIEL 1 – 21

1 visions of four flying animals, wheels, throne
2 Ezk sent to Israel, whether they listen or not
3 he eats scroll; 7 days' silence; he's a watchman

CALL

4 Ezk acts out prophecy of siege, exile, famine
5 "shave head, burn hair" – ⅓ die, ⅓ killed &c
6 altars, idolaters to be violently destroyed
7 riches, idolatry, will soon end; panic, confusion
8 vision: Ezk enters Temple thro' wall, sees idolatry
9 faithful marked on forehead; corpses in Temple
10 flying animals; fire on Jer^m; glory leaves Temple
11 25 men condemned; exiles promised new heart
12 Ezk acts out flight through wall as refugee
13 *v* prophets who say all is well; *v* magic wristbands
14 even Noah, Daniel, Job couldn't save the land
15 Jerusalem is like a useless vine
16 J^m an unfaithful wife; punishment, restoration
17 parable of cedar branch, vine, and two eagles
18 the one who sins will die, not his children
19 Israel likened to captive lions and a burnt vine
20 history reviewed; God will restore; fire in south
21 God's sword; sword of Babylon *v* Israel, Ammon

PUNISHMENT FOR JERUSALEM

EZEKIEL 22 – 48

22 Jer^m, city of blood, immorality, & oppression

23 Samaria, Jerusalem have behaved like prostitutes

24 J^m, foul as a rusty pot, is doomed; Ezk's wife dies

25 *v Ammon, Moab, Edom, Philistines*

26 *Tyre*'s rich trading centre will be a bare rock

27 funeral song for Tyre and its varied merchandise

28 *v* king of Tyre; *v Sidon;* Israel to return from exile

29 *Egypt:* "we made Nile!" but Babylon will conquer

30 Nebuchadnezzar to defeat and scatter Egypt

31 Egypt is like a proud cedar, will go to the dead

32 Pharaoh, Assyria, Edom, go to world of dead

33 watchman, God is just (Ezk 3, 18); J^m falls

34 *v* shepherds of Israel; good shepherd, covenant

35 *Edom* condemned for opposing Israel

36 Israel to be fertile; God will give new heart, spirit

37 dry bones live again; 2 sticks (Judah, Israel)

38 vast army of Gog (ungodly nations) to be defeated

39 Gog's weapons & men to be destroyed; Israel restored

40 plans for new Temple, outer & inner courtyards

41 Holy Place: walls, outer measurements; altar

42 buildings where priests are to eat the offerings

43 God's glory returns to Temple; altar consecrated

44 Levites, priests, can enter; rules, prohibitions

45 the land divided; use honest measures; festivals

46 role of prince & people in festivals; the kitchens

47 healing river flows from Temple; Israel's frontiers

48 the land divided; city gates; "the Lord is there"

MESSAGES FOR THE NATIONS (chapters 25–32)

PROMISES OF HOPE (chapters 33–39)

RESTORED TEMPLE, WORSHIP, & NATION (chapters 40–48)

DANIEL

1   4 exiles in Babylon go on vegetarian diet
2   Daniel: "dream of statue means 4 empires"
3   Daniel's friends saved from furnace, promoted
4   Daniel: "dream of tree means Neb will go mad"
5   Daniel explains writing on wall at Belshaz's feast
6   Daniel disobeys decree *v* prayer, put in lions' den
7   Dan's vision of 4 animals, 10+1 horns, judgement
8   Daniel's vision: ram (Media, Persia), goat (Greece)
9   Daniel's confession: holy city to be free in 490 yrs
10 fighter *v* Persia and Greece speaks to Daniel
11 Syria-Egypt war; Awful Horror in Temple (11:31)
12 angel predicts End when dead will live again

VISIONS

HOSEA

1   Hosea's unfaithful wife Gomer, and children
2   God is angry but still loves his unfaithful people
3   Hosea told to remarry his unfaithful wife
4   God accuses corrupt priests, idolatrous people
5   God will punish his sinful people with war
6   false repentance; God wants love, not sacrifice
7   corrupt nation seeks help from Egypt, Assyria
8   Israel made idols, will reap storm of oppression
9   Israel to be punished by exile; children to suffer
10 Israel's golden bull and king will be destroyed
11 God's love: "how can I give you up, Israel?"
12 Israel must return to God or be punished
13 men kiss idols! Samaritans rebelled & will be punished
14 return to the Lord! God will heal them

JOEL

1 locusts destroy crops; no pasture for cattle

2 repent before Day of the Lord; Spirit promised

3 nations in Valley of Judgement; future blessings

AMOS

1 Israel's neighbours condemned for repeated sins

2 ditto; Israelites oppress poor and godly

3 God's only nation; he uses prophets; *v* Samaria

4 women who oppress poor, then worship, warned

5 fall of Israel promised; *v* worship with injustice

6 those who enjoy luxurious life will suffer defeat

7 Amos pleads; God relents; Amos' defence *v* Amaziah

8 basket of fruit; profiteering punished by famine

9 none will escape; future restoration promised

OBADIAH

Edom turned *v* Israelite brothers, to be destroyed

JONAH

1 Jonah disobeys God's call, flees; thrown into sea

2 Jonah's prayer and promise from inside fish

3 J obediently preaches in Nineveh, people repent

4 Jonah resents God's mercy to Nineveh

MICAH

1 God will punish idolatry of Samaria, Jerusalem
2 social injustice; people say "don't preach!"
3 rulers oppress people, prophets promise peace
4 swords to ploughs; Israel will return from exile
5 deliverer from Bethlehem; idols to be destroyed
6 God wants justice, love, humility, not sacrifices
7 tho' dishonest, corrupt, God will save & forgive you

NAHUM

1 Nineveh can't escape punishment; message of hope
2 attack and violent capture of Nineveh described
3 corpses piled high; fortresses fall easily

HABAKKUK

1 why does God let Babylon punish Judah?
2 write: "God hates greed, murder, drink, idols"
3 God has all power; I'll wait, he is my saviour

ZEPHANIAH

1 day of God's judgement on Jerusalem is near
2 turn to God; surrounding nations to be punished
3 God will cleanse Jerusalem; sing! punishment is over

HAGGAI

1 we've sown much, harvested little; build Temple
2 beauty of Temple; defilement; Zerubbabel

ZECHARIAH

1 8 visions: *1* horses patrol the earth; *2* horns

2 *3* measuring Jerusalem; (God recalls exiles)

3 *4* high priest, accused by Satan, is cleansed

4 *5* gold lamp-stand and two olive trees

5 *6* flying scroll; *7* woman in basket

6 *8* four chariots – crown Joshua as the Branch

7 insincere fasting; exile a punishment for sin

8 10 promises that Jerusalem will be restored

9 *v* nations; Zion's King comes; Jerusalem restored

10 *v* superstition; God will save Judah and Israel

11 good shepherd replaced by a worthless one

12 Jerusalem feared by enemies, will mourn victim

13 end of false prophets; kill God's shepherd!

14 Jerusalem captured; plague hits Jer^m's enemies

8 VISIONS (bracket spanning verses 1–6)

MALACHI

1 God loves Jacob, rejects imperfect offerings

2 priests break covenant; husbands unfaithful

3 God sends messenger; robbing God in tithes

4 wicked burn on Day of the Lord; Elijah will come

MATTHEW 1 – 13

	1	Jesus' ancestors – Abraham, Boaz, David to Joseph	
		angel tells Joseph to marry Mary; Jesus born	
	2	star leads wise men to king Herod and baby Jesus	
		escape to Egypt; Herod kills 2-yr olds; J&M return	
1	3	John the Baptist's life-style and preaching	*3*
		John baptizes Jesus; "this is my own dear Son"	
1	4	temptations; Jesus' first preaching in Galilee	*4*
		Jesus calls 4 fishermen, preaches, **heals sick**	*5, 6*
	5	how to be happy; salt, light; the law will stay	*6, 14*
		"it was said…but I say…"; be perfect!	*16, 6*
	6	do your giving, prayer, fasting, in private;	*11*
		riches in heaven; don't worry about food, clothes	*12*
	7	don't judge; ask, seek, knock; narrow & wide gates	*6, 11*
		by their fruits; "Lord, Lord!"; *house on rock*	*6, 13*
1	8	Jesus **heals leper, officer's servant, & others**	*5, 7, 4*
4, 5		**calms storm; heals Gerasene men with evil spirits**	*8*
2	9	**paralytic;** Jesus calls Matthew; fasting; *patch; wine*	*5*
5		**official's daughter, woman; 2 blind men, &c**	*8*
3, 6, 13	10	12 called & sent; Jesus predicts persecution	*6, 9, 21*
		whom to fear; Jesus divides; rewards for welcome	*12, 14*
	11	John the Baptist's messengers; Jesus praises John	*7*
		fate of unbelieving Galilee; "come to me"	*10*
2, 3	12	corn on sabbath; **paralytic;** Jesus is the Servant	*6*
3, 8		Beelzebul; no sign; evil spirit returns; Jesus' mother	*11, 6*
4	13	*sower;* "why parables?"; *weeds; mustard seed*	*8, 13*
6		*yeast; treasure; pearl; net;* Jesus rejected at Nazareth	*13, 4*

Note: MIRACLES are printed in **bold type**
PARABLES are printed in *italics*

MATTHEW 14 – 28

THE LIFE OF JESUS

years before Christ	JESUS	EMPERORS OF ROME	RULERS IN PALESTINE		
			JUDEA	GALILEE	ITUREA
40					
			37 HEROD THE GREAT		
30					
		27 CAESAR AUGUSTUS	HEROD THE GREAT		
20					
10					
	6? birth		4 ARCHELAUS	4 HEROD ANTIPAS	4 HEROD PHILIP
years of our Lord					
	6? 1st Passover at Jerusalem		6		
10					
		14 TIBERIUS			
20					
			26 PONTIUS PILATE		
30	30* } 3-year ministry 33**				34
			36		
		37		39	

AD 30 - 33 – THE MINISTRY OF JESUS

	JESUS' TRAVELLING MINISTRY	JESUS' VISITS TO JERUSALEM	
		Festival	*Reference*
29	(John the Baptist begins ministry) baptism in Jordan		
30	Galilee *(Mark 1-6, John 1,2)*	Passover	*John 2:13*
	Samaria *(John 4:3-4)*		
31	Galilee	Booths	*John 5:1*
	Galilee, Tyre & Sidon	Passover	*John 6:4*
32	Caesarea Philippi *(Mark 7-9)*	Booths	*John 7:2*
	Galilee	Dedication	*John 10:22*
33	Judea	Passover (crucifixion & resurrection)	

Notes: Owing to changes in calculating the calendar, the year of Jesus' birth is thought to have been about 6 BC (Before Christ), but exact dates, even years, are generally unknown. AD means "in the year of our Lord" (Latin: Anno Domini).

* 15th year of Tiberius (Luke 3:1)

** in AD 33 the Feast of Passover fell on a Friday

MARK

PARABLES IN MATTHEW, MARK & LUKE

	Mat	*Mrk*	*Luk*
dishonest manager			16
faithful servant	24		12
fig-tree 1	24	13	21
2			13
fishing net	13		
good Samaritan			10
great feast			14
growing seed		4	
hidden treasure	13		
house on rock	7		6
lost coin			15
lost sheep	18		15
lost (prodigal) son			15
mustard seed	13	4	13
new patch	9	2	5
new wine	9	2	5
pearl	13		
persevering widow			18
Pharisee & tax-collector			18
rich fool			12
rich man & Lazarus			16
servants & absent master	25		19
sheep & goats	25		
sower	13	4	8
ten girls	25		
three loaves			11
two sons	21		
unforgiving servant	18		
watchful servants			12
wedding feast	22		
weeds	13		
wicked tenants	21	12	20
workers in vineyard	20		
yeast	13		13

MIRACLES IN THE FOUR GOSPELS

	Mat	*Mrk*	*Luk*	*Jhn*
Healing				
blind men: 1	9			
2		8		
3				9
4*	12			
5	20	10	18	
centurion's servant	8		7	
cripple			13	
daughter at Tyre	15	7		
dead people raised:				
Jairus' daughter	9	5	8	
Lazarus				11
widow's son at Nain			7	
deaf mute		7		
dropsy			14	
evil spirit possession:				
1 in synagogue		1	4	
2 Gerasa	8	5	8	
3 dumb	9			
4 blind*, dumb	12		11	
5 epileptic boy	17	9	9	
leper	8	1	5	
lepers, ten			17	
Malchus' ear			22	
man at pool of Bethesda				5
official's son				4
paralysed hand	12	3	6	
paralytic carried by four	9	2	5	
Peter's mother-in-law	8	1	4	
woman's haemorrhage	9	5	8	
Other miracles				
calming storm	8	4	8	
catch of fish: 1			5	
2				21
feeding of 4,000	15	8		
5,000	14	6	9	6
fig-tree	21			
Temple tax	17			
walking on water	14	6		6
water into wine				2

* same miracle

LUKE 1 – 12

	1	to Theoph[s]; Gabriel promises birth of J[n], Jesus	
		song of Mary; John born, named; song of Zechariah	
	2	Jesus born; shepherds see angels; purification	
		Simeon, Anna; Jesus' first Passover in Jerusalem	
3	3	John the Baptist on repentance, social & moral issues	1
3, 1		John baptizes Jesus; Jesus' ancestors	
4, 13	4	temptation; Jesus rejected at Nazareth	1, 6
8		**man with evil spirit; Peter's mother-in-law, &c**	1
4, 8, 9	5	Jesus calls disciples; **catch of fish; heals paralytic**	1, 2
9		calls Levi; fasting; *new patch, new wine*	
12, 10	6	corn on sabbath; **paralysed hand;** J chooses 12	2, 3
4, 5, 7		how to be happy; love enemies; judging; fruit	
8	7	Jesus **heals centurion's servant; widow's son**	
11		John the Baptist's messengers; Jesus anointed	
13, 8	8	*sower;* lamp & bowl; J's mother; **J calms storm**	3, 4, 8
8, 9		**Gerasene; Jairus' daug[tr]; woman's haemorrhage**	5
14, 16	9	12 sent; **5,000;** P[t] "You are Messiah"; J's death (1)	6, 8
17, 8		transfiguration; **boy;** Jesus predicts death (2)	8, 9
11	10	72 sent; unbelieving Galilee; 72 return with joy	
		good Samaritan; Jesus visits Mary & Martha	
6, 12	11	prayer; *3 loaves;* Beelzebul; evil spirit returns	3, 12
12, 23		no sign; Pharisees are hypocrites, inconsistent	12
10, 6	12	whom to fear; *rich fool;* don't worry about food	
24, 10, 16		servants – watchful, faithful; Jesus divides	

LUKE 13 – 24

JOHN 1 – 10

1   God, the Word, becomes flesh; Jⁿ baptizes Jesus

     Jesus calls Andrew, Peter, Philip, Nathanael

2   wedding at Cana – Jesus **turns water into wine**

     Jesus cleanses Temple: "I'll rebuild it in 3 days"

3   "be born again"; judgement if we reject the light

     John the Baptist speaks of Jesus: "he's from heaven"

4   Jesus & Samaritan woman at well; true worship

     Jesus says he is Messiah; **he heals official's son**

5   Jesus **heals sick man at pool of Bethesda**

     Jesus' right to give life; his deeds prove his authority

6   Jesus **feeds 5000, walks on water;** many seek him

     J is bread of life; "eat my flesh" – hard teaching

7   J's brothers; he goes to Jᵐ for festival of shelters

     people question Jesus' teaching, miracles, origin

8   Jesus & adulteress; "light of world…I am he"

     "if Son sets you free"; Jesus & Abraham, "I am"

9   **J heals blind man;** Pharisees question him & parents

     "I was blind, now I see"; blindness of Pharisees

10   *shepherd & thief;* good shepherd dies for sheep

     feast of dedication; attempt to stone, arrest Jesus

JOHN 11 – 21

11 Lazarus dies; "I am the resurrection & the life"
    Jesus calls **Laz to life;** "one must die for people"

12 Jesus anointed, enters J^m; "grain of wheat dies"
    J to be lifted up; Isaiah's prophecy of unbelief

13 Jesus washes disciples' feet, predicts betrayal
    Judas takes bread, goes out; "you'll deny me"

14 "I'll prepare place; way, truth, life; greater works;
    another Helper; peace; I'll leave & come back"

15 Jesus the real vine; branch in vine bears fruit
    "world hated me, will hate you; Helper will come"

16 "if I go, Helper will come & lead you into truth;
    you won't see me; ask, receive; world defeated"

17 Jesus' high priestly prayer: "I've given message,
    sent disciples into world; give safety, unity"

18 Jesus arrested; trial before Annas; Peter's denial
    Pilate examines Jesus; people choose Barabbas

19 "he's innocent, but crucify him!" Pilate's authority
    Jesus crucified; wine; his side pierced; burial

20 women, Peter, John at empty grave; Jesus appears
    to Mary Magdalene, 10 disciples, also to Thomas

21 and to 7 disciples at lake; catch of 153 big fish
    "do you love me?" how Peter, John will die

THE JOURNEYS OF PAUL

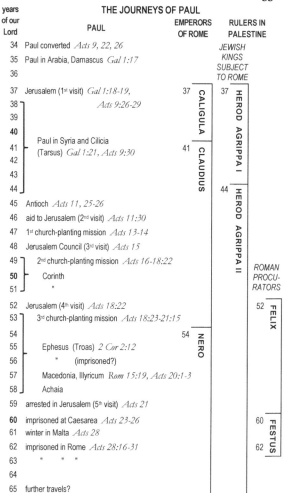

years of our Lord	PAUL	EMPERORS OF ROME	RULERS IN PALESTINE
34	Paul converted *Acts 9, 22, 26*		*JEWISH KINGS SUBJECT TO ROME*
35	Paul in Arabia, Damascus *Gal 1:17*		
36			
37	Jerusalem (1st visit) *Gal 1:18-19,*	37	37
38	*Acts 9:26-29*	CALIGULA	HEROD AGRIPPA I
39			
40			
41	Paul in Syria and Cilicia	41	
42	(Tarsus) *Gal 1:21, Acts 9:30*	CLAUDIUS	
43			
44			44
45	Antioch *Acts 11, 25-26*		HEROD AGRIPPA II
46	aid to Jerusalem (2nd visit) *Acts 11:30*		
47	1st church-planting mission *Acts 13-14*		
48	Jerusalem Council (3rd visit) *Acts 15*		
49	2nd church-planting mission *Acts 16-18:22*		
50	Corinth		
51	"		*ROMAN PROCU-RATORS*
52	Jerusalem (4th visit) *Acts 18:22*		52
53	3rd church-planting mission *Acts 18:23-21:15*		FELIX
54		54	
55	Ephesus (Troas) *2 Cor 2:12*	NERO	
56	" (imprisoned?)		
57	Macedonia, Illyricum *Rom 15:19, Acts 20:1-3*		
58	Achaia		
59	arrested in Jerusalem (5th visit) *Acts 21*		
60	imprisoned at Caesarea *Acts 23-26*		60 FESTUS
61	winter in Malta *Acts 28*		
62	imprisoned in Rome *Acts 28:16-31*		62
63	" " "		
64			
65	further travels?		

Note: Some scholars put Paul's conversion in AD 37

ACTS

1	"wait for Spirit"; ascension; Judas replaced	
2	Peter's sermon & call to repentance; church life	
3	**Pt heals lame man;** sermon at Temple gate	CHURCH IN JERUSALEM
4	Pt & John before Council; believers pray, share	
5	Ananias, Sapphira; **angel opens gate;** Gamaliel	
6	7 deacons to administer aid; Stephen arrested	
7	Stephen's summary of Jewish history; stoned	
8	Saul attacks church; Philip in Samaria; Ethiopn	JUDEA & SAMARIA
9	Saul meets Christ, preaches him; Aeneas, Dorcas	
10	Peter's vision; Cornelius saved, receives Spirit	
11	Peter reports to Jerm; evangelism at Antioch	
12	James killed, **angel releases Peter;** Herod's death	
13	Barnabas & Saul preach in: Cyprus, Ant/Pisidia,	
14	Iconium, Lystra (stoned), return to Ant/Syria	PAUL'S JOURNEYS 1 _ 2 _ 3
15	Jerm Council allows Paul's ministry to Gentiles	
16	Paul, Tim, Silas to Philippi; prison, earthquake	
17	riot in Thessalonica, Berea; Pls Athens sermon	
18	Corinth – vision, trial, vow, to Jm, Apollos in Eph	
19	Eph – sons of Sceva; silversmiths lead protest	
20	Macedonia, Troas; farewell to Eph church elders	
21	Agabus' prophecy; Pl sees Jas, arrested after riot	
22	Paul tells of conversion, call; he's Roman citizen	PAUL TRIED & SENT TO ROME
23	Paul divides Council; plot v Pl; sent to Caesarea	
24	trial before Felix – Tertul's accusn, Pls defence	
25	trial before Festus; Paul appeals to Caesar	
26	Pl tells Agrippa of his conversion, work, belief	
27	Pl sails to Cyprus, Crete; storm, wreck at Malta	
28	3 mths in Malta; Pl arrives in Rome & preaches	

ROMANS

1 Paul plans to visit Rome; human sin, God's anger

2 religious people can be as guilty as unbelievers

3 none are saved by good deeds, only by faith

4 how Abraham was put right with God by faith

SALVATION

5 results of being right with God; Adam & Christ

6 X[ns] dare not sin lest we become slaves of evil

7 dead to sin & law, yet inner conflict goes on

8 live in the Spirit, expect glory! God is on our side

HOLINESS

9 God's choice of Israel not unjust; Christ a "stone"

10 preaching leads to saving faith in Christ

11 Israel not rejected; Gentiles blessed through Israel

ISRAEL

12 offer yourselves, use gifts; good overcomes evil

13 civic duties; love fulfils law; put on Christ

14 freedom & responsibility in doubtful issues

15 help others as Christ did; Paul's aim to visit Rome

16 greetings; warning *v* divisions; praise God!

RULES FOR CHRISTIAN LIFE

1 CORINTHIANS 1 – 4

1 *v* divisions; preaching the cross seems "foolish"

2 Paul weak; he teaches wisdom to spiritual people

3 Paul & Apollos – building on Christ's foundation

4 apostles are servants, weak; Paul is Cor[ns]' father

DIVISIONS

1 CORINTHIANS 5 – 16

5 Paul deals with a case of immorality at Corinth

6 *v* lawsuits among Xⁿˢ; sex sin hurts your body

7 duties in marriage; non-Xⁿ partners; single life

8 food offered to idols; protect sensitive brothers

9 pay pastors, but not Paul! "all things to all men"

10 *v* idolatry (Num 25) & food offered to idols

11 women in church; order at Lord's Supper

12 spiritual gifts; Christians are part of Christ's body

13 love greater than any other gift

14 use of tongues & prophecy; conduct of worship

15 Christ really rose; we'll rise too, with a spiritual body

16 regular giving; Paul's travel plans; greetings

PROBLEMS IN CHURCH

GIFTS

2 CORINTHIANS

1 Paul's sufferings; why his visit was postponed

2 forgive the sinner! anxiety & triumph at Troas

3 you're my "letter"; new covenant; veil removed

4 Paul's preaching not cunning; we're clay pots!

5 heavenly hope; Xⁿˢ are made new, friends of God

6 Paul's hardships; don't join unbelievers

7 Titus reports repentance after earlier letter

8 Titus to arrange collection for Christians in Judea

9 Macedonians' gifts; rewards of cheerful giving

10 Paul is not "humble at Corinth, proud in letters"

11 false apostles; Paul's weaknesses & sufferings

12 Paul's vision & thorn; his concern for Corinthians

13 Paul plans to visit Corinth & confront sinners

CHRISTIAN MINISTRY

GIVING

PAUL & CRITICS

GALATIANS

1 Jesus died for our sins, that's the only gospel;
  Paul's call and early Christian life
2 P^l agreed with leaders in Jer^m that X^{ns} need not be
  circumcised, but clashed with P^t; faith, not law, saves
3 Abr$^{m's}$ faith; curse of law; law reveals our wrongdoing
4 be sons not slaves! (e.g. sons of Sarah, Hagar)
5 be free! *v* circumcision; work of flesh and Spirit
6 care for each other; sow, reap; boast about cross

EPHESIANS

1 God chose, saved, called us; prayer for readers
2 our old life; grace saves; Jews & Gentiles are one
3 Paul reveals God's secret, prays all may know God
4 roles in church; put off old, put on new way of X^n life
5 *v* immoral life, talk; wives' and husbands' duties
6 children, parents, slaves' duties; armour of God; pray!

PHILIPPIANS

1 may you grow! in prison for Christ, I live for Christ
2 Christ's humble example; X$^{ns'}$ holy life; P$^{l's}$ helpers
3 Paul left "religion" for Christ, seeks the goal
4 unity, joy, prayer, right thinking; thanks for gift

COLOSSIANS

1 prayer of thanks; X^t the creator, reconciler; P^l a servant
2 be firm in faith! live in Christ and reject legalism
3 put old life off, new life on; duties in family etc
4 pray for us; Christian behaviour; greetings

1 THESSALONIANS

1 their conversion and faith known in Macedonia
2 Paul's behaviour and preaching; their response
3 Paul, anxious, sent Timothy to get news of them
4 holy life; dead will rise first when Christ returns
5 Day of the Lord; care for pastors; rules for church

2 THESSALONIANS

1 their faith growing; judgment when Christ comes
2 Wicked One comes before Day of the Lord
3 pray for us; work hard, as Paul does

1 TIMOTHY

1 *v* false teaching; how sinful Paul was saved
2 rules for worship: prayer, dress, women
3 qualifications for pastors & other church officers
4 *v* false teaching; rules for Timothy as a church leader
5 respect elders; support widows & church leaders
6 slaves, serve well! *v* greed; faithful service

2 TIMOTHY

1 use your gifts; Christian certainty; a cheerful friend
2 Christian like soldier, approved workman; *v* disputes
3 vices in last days; persecution; study the Bible
4 keep preaching; Paul's prize; Christians deserted P[l]

TITUS

1 qualifications for church officers; *v* false teaching
2 sound teaching and sound behaviour
3 God saved us though fools; *v* disputes; be useful

PHILEMON

Paul sends back runaway slave, now converted

HEBREWS

1 how God has spoken; Son better than angels

2 great salvation: Jesus suffered, died, as a real man

3 Jesus greater than Moses; warning *v* unbelief

4 God's rest; sharp Word; high priest who cares

5 Christ greater than other priests; you need milk

6 warning *v* apostasy; God's promise an anchor

7 Melchizedek's priesthood prior to Levitical ones

8 Christ's covenant, priesthood better than old one

9 sacrifices repeated, but Christ's death once for all

10 Christ died for sin, so draw near! *v* deliberate sin

11 faith at work in OT saints, yet not perfect

12 run race, accept discipline; Zion, not Sinai

13 Christian duties; Jesus the same; Christian sacrifices

OUR PRIEST

OUR SACRIFICE

JAMES

1 ask for wisdom; temptation; hearing and doing

2 prejudice *v* poor; faith without works is dead

3 tongue is a fire; wisdom from above

4 choose world or God! judging; "if God wills"

5 warning to rich; patience; pray; confess sins

1 PETER

1 Xns are born again, tested, holy, bought by Christ

2 Christ the Stone; Xn way of life; suffer as Xt did

3 beauty of wives; suffer for the right; baptism

4 changed lives; use talents; expect persecution

5 elders' duties; God cares! devil like a lion

2 PETER

1 keep growing; Peter saw Christ's glory; prophecy

2 some deny Christ, reject authority, insult, boast

3 Christ delays his coming to give chance to repent

1 JOHN

1 John saw Christ; walk in light; confess sin

2 *1 our love & obedience; v* Enemy of Christ

3 *2 those born of God don't sin; 3 gift of Spirit*

4 *4 Christ came in flesh; 5 Jesus is Son of God*

5 *6 obedience;* witness of Christ; *7 answered prayer*

7 WAYS TO BE SURE

2 JOHN

don't accept any who deny Christ came in flesh

3 JOHN

Gaius is hospitable; Doitrephes opposes John

JUDE

woe to ungodly men; you persevere; doxology

REVELATION

1 John on isle of Patmos sees Son of Man, 7 lamps

2 letters to Ephesus, Smyrna, Pergamum, Thyatira

3 letters to Sardis, Philadelphia, Laodicea

|LETTERS|

4 24 elders & 4 animals worship God in heaven

5 Lamb seems killed, opens scroll; new songs

6 6 seals opened – visions of war, persecution

7 144,000 of Israel, uncountable crowd, in heaven

8 7th seal: 4 trumpets herald partial destruction

9 5th trumpet, locusts; 6th, one-third mankind killed

10 angel gives John little scroll to eat: "proclaim!"

11 measure Temple; 2 witnesses die; 7th trumpet

|7 SEALS, 7 TRUMPETS|

12 dragon pursuing woman & child thrown to earth

13 1st beast's 42-month reign; mark of 2nd beast

14 song of 144,000; 3 angels' messages; earth reaped

15 song at glassy sea; 7 angels from heavenly temple

16 7 plagues or bowls of God's anger poured out

|7 BOWLS|

17 woman (= Babylon) & beast oppose Lamb

18 Babylon (= Rome) falls – angels, kings, traders lament

19 wedding feast of Lamb; Word of God on horse

20 Satan bound 1,000 years; white judgement throne

21 new heaven, earth; "God with man"; new Jerusalem

22 river from throne; Jesus coming; don't add to book

ALPHABETICAL INDEX OF BIBLE BOOKS

About the author

Born in Feltham in 1928, Peter Barker first read the Bible daily as a choir-boy at Winchester Cathedral. National Service sent him to East Africa, where listening to radio broadcasts from Nairobi Cathedral led him to give his life to the Lord Jesus.

Peter returned to the UK, read history at Oxford and then went to work as a journalist and teacher in Ghana until he felt the call to preach the gospel full-time. He offered himself to the Presbyterian Church of Ghana and, following a year of part-time study in London, returned to Ghana to study privately for his BD at Trinity Theological College in Kumasi. He led a congregation in Accra for three years and then worked for the Ghana Christian Council, founding the Asɛmpa Publishing house in 1968.

In 1985, Peter and his family returned to the UK where he served four URC congregations in the East Midlands, followed by St Andrew's URC, Cheam; in both places inspiring many with his enthusiasm and extraordinary breadth of knowledge.

A man of God, an apostle, a wise mentor and a tireless evangelist: Peter Barker was all of these and more. May you be inspired by the work he did in producing this book.

HELPFUL VERSES
a personal selection by Laura Barker

In these few pages are lists of some of the helpful verses from the Bible which I've discovered over the years; how I wish I'd discovered them all much earlier in my Christian life. That's why I want to share them with you. No doubt you will add some of your own – there are many more to find!

But how are you going to know what's in here and so be able to refer to it when you want to find a particular verse? A bit of hard work, initially, is the only answer. That means going through these pages with your Bible to find the verses – and I suggest you mark or underline them in your Bible.

The more often you look up a verse the easier it will become to find it – you will begin to remember whether the verse you want is in the Old or New Testament, then perhaps which book it is in – even if the chapter and verse escapes you!

Genesis
2:24 God's plan for man & wife
3:1-19 man's fall, disobedience
15:6 Abram made right with
　　God through faith
28:22 give one tenth to God
　(also Deu 14:22, 26:12, Lev 27:30)

Exodus
3:14 God's name *(also John 8:58)*
18:17-23 principle of delegating
19:5 we are God's treasured
　　possession
20:1-17 the ten commandments
　(also Deu 5:6-21)
33:11 God & Moses' face-to-
　　face relationship
　(also Num 12:8)

Leviticus
18:22 about homosexuality
　(also Rom 1:27)
19:1 be holy, because God is
　　holy *(also 20:7-8, 26)*
19:31 don't consult mediums
　(also Deu 18:10-11, Isa 8:19)
24:17-21 a life for a life
27:30 a tithe belongs to God
　(also Gen 28:22, Deu 14:22, 26:12)

Numbers
6:24-26 the Lord bless you...
12:8 God & Moses' face-to-
　　face relationship
　(also Exo 33:11)
23:19 God is not a man that he
　　should lie

Deuteronomy
5:6-21 the ten commandments
   (also Exo 20:1-17)
6:4-5 love God with all your
   heart, soul & strength
   (also Mat 22:37)
8:11-20 don't forget God
10:12-13 what God requires
   (also Mic 6:8)
14:22 give one tenth to God
   (also 26:12, Gen 28:22, Lev 27:30)
18:10-11 don't consult mediums
   (also Lev 19:31, Isa 8:19)
30:11-20 choose life
31:6 do not be afraid, he will
   never leave you
33:27 God's everlasting arms
   underneath us

Joshua
1:6-9 be strong, keep God's law
24:15 choose whom you serve

Judges
6:36-40 Gideon & the fleece

Ruth
1:16 your God is my God

1 Samuel
3:1-10 the call of Samuel
16:7 God looks at the heart

2 Samuel
24:24 don't give God something
   which costs nothing

1 Kings
3:9 Solomon asks for wisdom

2 Kings

1 Chronicles
29:14 everything we give comes
   from God

2 Chronicles

Ezra

Nehemiah
8:10 the joy of the Lord is our
   strength

Esther

Job
19:25 I know my Redeemer lives
23:10 after testing, I shall come
   forth as gold
33:14-20 how God speaks to us

Psalms
8:3-4 what is man that God
   should care for him
19:1 heavens declare God's glory
23 the Lord is my shepherd
34:8 taste & see the Lord is good
37:3-5 trust in him
42:1 as the deer pants…so my
   soul pants for God
46:10 be still & know I am God
51 David's confession of sin
91 God's protection
103:11-12 God's love &
   forgiveness
111:10 fear of the Lord is the
   beginning of wisdom
   (also Pro 9:10)

Psalms (cont.)

119:11 God's word hidden in
our hearts
119:105 God's word is a lamp
121:1 I will lift up my eyes
127:1 unless the Lord builds
the house
139 we cannot escape God – he
knows us

Proverbs

3:5-6 trust in the Lord with *all*
your heart
9:10 fear of the Lord is the
beginning of wisdom
(also Psa 111:10)
15:1 a gentle answer turns away
wrath
22:6 train a child
(also 3:11-12, 19:18)
31:10-31 the capable wife

Ecclesiastes

3 a time for everything
12:13 whole duty of man – fear
God & keep commands

Song of Songs

8:6-7 what love is

Isaiah

1:18 sins, as scarlet, shall be
white as snow
2:4 swords turned into ploughshares *(also Mic 4:3)*
6:8 here I am, send me
7:14 the virgin will be with child
8:19 don't consult mediums
(also Lev 19:31, Deu 18:10-11)

9:6-7 to us a child is born –
wonderful counsellor etc
26:3 God's promise of peace
29:13 false worship
30:15 real trust in God
30:20-21 how God guides us
through hard times
35:5-6 eyes of the blind opened
40 Messiah prophecy & what
God is like
41:10 do not be afraid
43:1-5 fear not, I am with you
43:25 promise of forgiveness
(also 44:22)
49:15-16 God never forgets us
53 the suffering servant
55:6 seek the Lord, call on him
55:9 God's ways are higher than
our ways
55:11 God's word will achieve
what he wants
58:6-7 fasting – God's pattern
59:2 sin separates us from God
61:1-3 Spirit of the Lord is on
me (Messiah prophecy)
64:6 our righteous acts are like
filthy rags
64:8 the potter & the clay
(also Jer 18:1-6)
65:17-25 new earth, heavens –
no more weeping

Jeremiah

9:24 if you boast, only that you
know God *(also 1 Cor 1:31)*
18:1-6 the potter & the clay
(also Isa 64:8)
29:11-13 God's plans for us, we
seek with *all* our heart

31:33-34 God's new promise to write his law on people's hearts & the promise of forgiveness

Lamentations
3:22-23 God's love is new every morning – great is his faithfulness

Ezekiel
34 good & bad shepherds & God's reaction
36:26-27 promise of a new heart
37:1-14 the valley of dry bones

Daniel
3:17-18 Daniel's friends trust God in the fiery furnace
6 in the lions' den

Hosea
6:6 God desires mercy not sacrifice *(also Psa 51:16)*

Joel
2:28-29 God will pour out his Spirit *(also Acts 2:17-18)*
3:10 ploughshares into swords

Amos
5:21-22 God is against formal religion

Obadiah

Jonah

Micah
4:3 swords turned into ploughshares *(also Isa 2:4)*

5:2 ruler will come from Bethlehem (Messiah prophecy)
6:8 what God requires of us *(also Deu 10:12-13)*

Nahum

Habakkuk
2:14 the earth will be filled with the knowledge of the Lord
3:17-18 though all fails, yet I will rejoice in the Lord

Zephaniah
3:17 God delights in us

Haggai

Zechariah
9:9 king riding on a donkey (Messiah prophecy)

Malachi
3:6-10 how we rob God

●●●

Matthew
4:1-11 Jesus tempted
5, 6, 7 beatitudes & sermon on the mount
18:15 if your brother sins against you…
18:20 where two or three are gathered together in Jesus' name – God is there
22:37 love God with all your heart, soul & mind *(also Deu 6:4-5)*
24 the 2nd coming of Christ

68

Mark

2:27 sabbath was made for man
6:5-6 no miracles because of
    lack of faith
7:8 human traditions pushed
    God's commands out
7:18-23 what makes us unclean
12:17 give to God/Caesar

Luke

5:32 Jesus did not come for the
    righteous but for sinners
6:37-38 don't judge/condemn
    others *(also Mat 7:1-2)*
10:41-42 Martha & Mary
14:27 whoever doesn't carry his
    cross can't be my disciple

John

1:12 those who believe are
    children of God
3:3 we need to be born again
3:16 God so loved the world –
    eternal life for believers
    (also 5:24, 6:40, 47, 54)
6:35 I am the bread of life – he
    who believes in me need
    never be hungry or thirsty
6:68 Jesus has words of life
8:12 I am the light of the world
8:32 the truth will set you free
8:58 before Abraham was, I am
    (also Exo 3:14)
10:7 I am the gate
10:11,14 I am the good shepherd
10:28 no one can snatch us
    away from Jesus *(cf. Heb 6:4)*
11:25 I am the resurrection &
    the life

11:35 Jesus wept
13:34 a new command: love one
    another
14:6 I am the way, the truth &
    the life
14:9 if we've seen Jesus, we've
    seen the Father
14:26 Counsellor (Holy Spirit)
    will teach & remind you
14:27 peace I leave with you
15:1 I am the true vine
15:13 greater love has no one…
16:23-24 ask in Jesus' name
(also 14:14)
16:33 I have overcome the world
17 Jesus' prayer
19:35 John's testimony so we
    may believe
20:30-31 words recorded so we
    may believe

Acts

2:1-4,17-18 Holy Spirit comes
(also Joel 2:28-29)
2:42-47 life of new believers
(also 4:32-35)
9:1-19 Saul's conversion on the
    road to Damascus
10 Peter in a Gentile house
12:6-11 Peter's miraculous
    escape from prison
20:32 word of God builds you up

Romans

1:16 God's power for salvation
1:27 about homosexuality
(also Lev 18:22)
3:20,22,28 righteousness comes
    through faith

5:1 peace with God

5:8 while we were still sinners, Christ died for us

6:23 the wages of sin is death, God's gift is eternal life

7:15 Paul's inward struggle

8:1 no condemnation for those in Christ Jesus

8:16 we are God's children

8:26 the Spirit helps us to pray

8:28 God works for the good of those who love him

8:38-39 nothing can separate us from God's love

10:9 if we confess Jesus is Lord & believe, we'll be saved

10:13-15 how can others believe … if they've not heard?

12:1 offer ourselves as living sacrifices

13:1 duties toward government

14:13 we mustn't be a stumbling block to others

1 Corinthians

1:31 boast only about knowing God *(also Jer 9:24)*

3:16 we are God's temple *(also 6:19)*

5:11 fellowship & discipline

6:12 everything permissible, but not everything is beneficial

7 marriage

9:22 Paul: all things to all men

10:13 no temptation beyond what we can bear

11:17-29 the Lord's supper

12 spiritual gifts; one body many parts

13 love

14 more on spiritual gifts

15 resurrection

2 Corinthians

1:4 we can comfort others with God's comfort

4:7 our treasure is in jars of clay

4:16 outwardly we are wasting away, but inwardly being renewed every day

5:10 appearing before the judgement seat

5:17-18 we are a new creation, in Christ reconciled to God

8:9-15 about giving

9:7 God loves a cheerful giver

12:7 Paul's thorn in the flesh

12:9 God's grace sufficient for us

13:14 the grace of our Lord Jesus

Galatians

2:16 justified by faith

2:20 crucified with Christ

3:28 all one in Christ

5:22-24 fruits of the Spirit

Ephesians

1:15-23 Paul's prayer for us

2:8-9 we are saved by grace through faith, not works

3:14-21 a prayer to him who will do more than we ask

4:15 speak the truth in love

4:22-24 put off old self, put on new self *(also Col 3:9-10)*

4:26 don't stay angry

5:22–6:4 wives/husbands, parents/children *(also Col 3:18-21)*

6:10-17 the armour of God

Philippians

1:6 confidence in God
1:21 for me, to live is Christ
2:5-8 imitate Christ's humility
2:9-11 at the name of Jesus,
     every knee should bow
3:7-10 knowing Jesus
4:4-7 rejoice, don't be anxious,
     the peace of God
4:8 whatever is true, noble, etc
4:12 I've learned to be content
4:13 I can do everything by the
     power that Christ gives

Colossians

1:9-12 Paul's prayer for us
1:15 Jesus is supreme
2:6-7 growing as a Christian
3:2 set our minds on things above
3:9-10 put off old self, put on
     new self *(also Eph 4:22-24)*
3:15-16 the peace of God in us
3:18-21 personal relationships
     (also Eph 5:22–6:4)

1 Thessalonians

3:12-13 Paul's prayer for us
4:13–5:3 the 2nd coming of Christ

2 Thessalonians

2:1-12 man of lawlessness
2:16-17 Paul's prayer for us

1 Timothy

1:15-16 Paul the worst sinner
1:18 fight the good fight
     (also 6:12, 2 Tim 4:7)
2:3-4 God wants *all* to know him
     (also 2 Pet 3:9)
2:5 one God, one mediator, Jesus

2:9-15 Paul's attitude to women
3:1-13 elders/deacons
     (also Titus 1:6-9, 1 Pet 5:1-4)
5:8 provide for the family
5:23 drink a *little* wine
6:10 the love of money is a root
     of all evil

2 Timothy

1:12 I know whom I've believed
2:2 entrust the gospel to reliable
     people
2:3-6 Christian life like being an
     athlete/soldier/farmer
2:15 we must correctly handle
     the word of truth
3:16 all scripture God-breathed
     for teaching, rebuking, etc
4:7 fight the good fight
     (also 1 Tim 1:18, 6:12)

Titus

1:6-9 elders/deacons
     (also 1 Tim 3:1-1, 1 Pet 5:1-4)
3:4-7 the gospel in a nutshell

Philemon

Hebrews

2:18 Jesus knows temptation
4:12 word of God like a sword
4:14-16 Jesus tempted, but sinless;
     our confidence in him
6:4-6 the possibility of losing
     salvation *(cf. John 10:28)*
7:25 Jesus saves completely
7:27 a once for all sacrifice
     (also 9:28)
10:4 impossible for animal
     sacrifice to save us

10:19-25 about confidence – we must draw near, hold on, not give up meeting together, encourage each other
11 by faith…
12:1-3 we must run the race & fix our eyes on Jesus
12:7-11 about discipline
13:8 Jesus is the same yesterday, today & for ever
13:17 obey leaders & authorities *(also 1 Pet 2:13)*
13:20-21 a prayer

James

1:2 coping with trials *(also 1:12)*
1:22 hear & *do* God's word
1:26 the tongue *(also 3:5-12)*
2:1-7 no favouritism
2:14-26 faith & deeds
4:7-8 resist devil, draw near God
4:13-16 planning the future
4:17 not doing good is sin
5:13-16 praying for the sick & confessing sin

1 Peter

1:6-7 testing our faith
2:2 our need to grow
2:9 we are a chosen people
2:13 obey the authorities *(also Heb 13:17)*
3:1-7 wives/husbands
3:15 we must be ready with an answer (about our faith)
4:12 don't be surprised at suffering
5:1-4 elders' responsibilities *(also 1 Tim 3:1-13, Titus 1:6-9)*
5:7 cast all our anxiety on him

2 Peter

1:5-7 how to grow in our faith
1:20-21 Scripture is God-inspired
3:9 God wants *all* to come to him *(also 1 Tim 2:3-4)*
3:10 the 2nd coming of Christ

1 John (the "we know" letter)

1:5-7 walking in the light
1:8-10 if we confess, he forgives
2:15 what love of the world is
3:2 we shall be like him
4:1 testing the spirits
4:4 God is greater than evil
4:16-18 God is love, perfect love drives out fear
5:11-12 he who has Son has life

2 John

10 don't welcome stranger who brings wrong teaching

3 John

Jude

24 God is able to keep us from falling

Revelation

1:7 the 2nd coming of Christ
2&3 letters to seven churches
3:20 behold I stand at the door & knock
7:9 a great multitude (*more* than 144,000)
7:15-17 about heaven, God will wipe away all tears *(also 21:4)*
22:13 I am the Alpha & Omega
22:18 don't add to or take away from this book

Notes